When Abundance Feels Like a Threat

When Abundance Feels Like a Threat

Matthew Petchinsky

1

When Abundance Feels Like a Threat: Healing the Hidden Fears of Enough

By: Matthew Petchinsky

Disclaimer

This guide explores the subconscious fears, patterns, and traumas that can sabotage a person's sense of financial security and safety. It is intended for educational and reflective purposes only. It is **not** a substitute for therapy, trauma counseling, financial planning, or legal advice. Readers who are navigating acute distress, clinical trauma, or serious financial/legal matters should seek appropriate professional guidance.

As the author, I want to be clear: I am not against abundance, wealth creation, or prosperity. In fact, I believe every person has the right to access abundance in a way that feels safe, grounded, and aligned with their deepest values. This work is not about rejecting abundance—it is about recognizing the hidden wounds, beliefs, and inherited fears that unconsciously block us from fully receiving and embodying it.

The exercises and reflections offered here are designed to bring awareness to those patterns so that readers may begin releasing what no longer serves them. By addressing money traumas, the intention is to clear space for healthier, more empowered, and more expansive relationships with wealth, rather than to diminish or deny the possibility of abundance itself.

Introduction

Do you sabotage your progress just when life feels stable? Do you find yourself taking three steps forward only to slide two steps back, especially when it comes to money, career, or security? If so, you may be carrying what I call an *abundance wound*.

Most of us think of financial trauma in terms of not having enough: the anxiety of bills piling up, the panic of an empty account, or the lingering memories of growing up in scarcity. But there is another layer, less discussed yet equally powerful—some people do not just fear lack; they fear *overflow*. For them, stability itself feels dangerous. A sense of security can trigger the same alarms in the brain as chaos. The moment life begins to feel steady, safe, or prosperous, something deep inside whispers, *This isn't right. This isn't safe. You don't deserve this.*

Why does this happen? Trauma rewires the brain and body to anticipate danger even in moments of peace. If you grew up in instability—where sudden losses, betrayals, or volatility defined your environment—your nervous system may have learned to equate safety with vulnerability. In other words, calm becomes suspicious, abundance becomes threatening, and "enough" feels like a trap waiting to collapse.

This book is about uncovering those hidden fears and patterns. It is not about teaching you how to "manifest" more money, nor is it about condemning abundance. I am not against prosperity; I believe deeply in our ability to create, hold, and expand wealth in ways that are life-giving and nourishing. But to truly receive abundance, we must first create inner safety—safety around peace, safety around stability, safety around the experience of *enough*.

Together, we will explore the psychology of sabotage: why people abandon opportunities, push away income, or unconsciously destabilize their lives when things are going well. We will also explore how to recognize these patterns, meet them with compassion, and slowly retrain the nervous system to hold security without fear. Through stories, exercises, and reflections, you will be guided not to chase abundance recklessly, but to welcome it in ways that feel sustainable and aligned with your truth.

This is not a book about quick fixes. It is a book about building new foundations. You will learn to spot the hidden triggers of money wounds, gently disarm the sabotaging behaviors they fuel, and cultivate the kind of grounded prosperity that endures.

Some people fear not having enough. Others fear what might happen if they finally do. This book is for both—for anyone who has ever felt unsafe with money, whether in scarcity or in plenty. By the end, my hope is that you will feel more at home in your relationship with financial peace, knowing that safety and abundance are not opposites, but partners.

Chapter 1: When Safety is Unfamiliar

Safety should feel natural. In theory, when our bills are paid, when the lights stay on, and when there is food in the pantry, we should breathe easier. Yet for many people, these moments of security feel strangely *unnatural.* Instead of relief, the nervous system tightens. Instead of gratitude, suspicion creeps in. Safety feels like the calm before a storm—and that storm always feels inevitable.

This is the paradox of trauma: it can make the unfamiliar feel unsafe, even when the unfamiliar is peace.

The Nervous System's Blueprint

Our bodies keep a record of the environments we grew up in. If those environments were unstable—financially, emotionally, or physically—our nervous system learned to anticipate chaos. Think of it like a survival algorithm: it runs in the background, predicting danger before it arrives.

When survival depends on constant vigilance, calm feels risky. For a child who never knew when the electricity might be cut off, when rent would be due, or when a parent's mood would shift without warning, safety was never steady. As adults, those early imprints continue to shape how we respond to financial stability.

To the trauma-wired brain, safety is not a resting place—it is a setup. It says: *Don't relax. Don't trust this. It won't last.*

The Fear of Letting Down Our Guard

Imagine standing guard for years at the edge of a fortress. Every noise, every shadow, every shift in the wind feels like a potential attack. Then one day, you're told: "It's safe now. You can come inside."

Would you walk in easily? Or would you wait at the gate, unable to believe the danger is gone?

This is what financial safety feels like for many. Having a savings account, a reliable job, or a paid-off debt is not experienced as victory. It's experienced as vulnerability. If you let your guard down, you fear you'll be blindsided. If you relax into safety, you fear the floor will collapse beneath you.

So the subconscious steps in with sabotage. Overspending, quitting a stable job abruptly, rejecting opportunities, or creating unnecessary conflict can serve as unconscious strategies to return to what feels familiar—instability.

Why We Mistake Safety for Danger

There are three common reasons why financial peace can feel threatening:

1. **Unfamiliarity** – If your baseline was scarcity or volatility, stability feels foreign. What's foreign often feels unsafe.
2. **Anticipation of Loss** – Abundance can trigger dread because your body remembers what it felt like to lose. The more you have, the more you fear losing.
3. **Identity Conflict** – Many internalize beliefs like *"I am poor,"* or *"People like me don't have money."* When reality challenges that identity, self-sabotage emerges to restore the familiar self-image.

The Hidden Costs of Sabotage

When safety is unfamiliar, sabotage may feel strangely comforting. A drained savings account, a missed bill, or another crisis may feel stressful, but at least it feels *known*. Known patterns—even painful ones—can provide a false sense of control.

But this cycle has costs. It erodes trust in yourself, drains energy, and perpetuates the very wounds you want to escape. The pattern whispers: *You can't handle safety. You don't deserve abundance.* And unless confronted, it repeats.

The First Step: Naming the Pattern

The good news is that patterns lose some of their power when named. By reading these words, you may already recognize yourself in them. Perhaps you've noticed how you resist calm, how you unconsciously create drama when life is steady, or how money slips away the moment it accumulates. Naming this is not a confession of weakness—it's an act of awareness.

Awareness opens the door to choice. You can begin to ask: *What does safety feel like in my body? What story do I tell myself when money is present? What fear rises when there is "enough"?*

This chapter is not about fixing the pattern in one stroke. It is about daring to notice it, sit with it, and admit that safety itself may feel unsafe.

A New Definition of Safety

To heal an abundance wound, we must redefine safety—not as a fragile pause between disasters, but as a foundation we can build upon. This redefinition does not erase trauma, but it rewrites our relationship to it.

Safety is not an illusion. It is not a trap. It is the steady ground on which abundance can stand. Learning to accept safety as *real* and *deserved* is the first step toward financial peace that lasts.

Reflection Prompt:

Think of a time when you experienced financial stability—perhaps when you had savings, a steady paycheck, or debts paid off. How did you feel in that moment? Relieved? Anxious? Suspicious? Write down your body's response. This reflection will help you begin noticing how safety registers in your system.

Chapter 2: Abundance Anxiety: The Fear of Enough

For many, the word *abundance* evokes joy, security, and possibility. Yet for others, abundance itself is terrifying. Not because they don't want it, but because holding "enough" feels dangerous. This is the essence of *abundance anxiety*: the fear that having more will make you a target, mark you as selfish, or expose you to inevitable loss.

When you've lived broke, your nervous system learns to normalize struggle. The absence of resources feels familiar, even survivable. But when resources finally arrive—whether in the form of money, security, or stability—your body may recoil. *This is too much. I shouldn't have this. Something bad is coming.*

Instead of relaxing into wealth, the impulse is to get rid of it. To overspend. To give it away too quickly. To make sure it doesn't linger long enough to draw unwanted attention.

When Abundance Feels Like a Target

Growing up with financial insecurity often imprints the belief that standing out is unsafe. If you had nicer clothes than your peers, you may have been bullied. If you had more food at lunch, you may have felt pressured to share. If you bought something new while your family still struggled, you may have been scolded.

As adults, these moments evolve into subconscious fears that abundance paints a bullseye on your back. Having savings may feel like announcing, *I'm hoarding. I'm selfish. Someone will resent me.* Buying something nice may trigger the thought, *People will judge me.* Even success itself can feel like exposure.

The result? Many unconsciously sabotage wealth to protect themselves. By staying broke, you stay invisible. By draining abundance, you remain unthreatening.

The Guilt We Inherit: Programmed Language

From a young age, many of us were programmed with subtle yet powerful language around money and resources:

- *"If you don't share, you're selfish."*
- *"If you have more, you should feel lucky."*
- *"Don't be greedy."*
- *"You should be grateful for what you have and not ask for more."*

On the surface, these phrases are framed as moral lessons. But underneath, they can teach children that having more than others is wrong. They build a psychological framework where abundance is equated with guilt, shame, or arrogance.

As adults, these programs run silently in the background. You may find yourself giving away more than you can afford, downplaying your achievements, or even rejecting financial opportunities—not out of true generosity, but out of guilt.

The Shame of Wanting More

When you've internalized these scripts, simply desiring more can feel shameful. Wanting abundance may feel like greed. Holding onto money may feel like betrayal. Asking for a raise, increasing your prices, or celebrating financial wins may feel like you are breaking some unwritten social contract.

This shame doesn't come from your authentic self—it comes from conditioning. But unless recognized, it will continue to sabotage your ability to feel safe with abundance.

The Cycle of "Getting Rid of Enough"
Here's how abundance anxiety often shows up in practice:

1. **Money Arrives.** A paycheck, a windfall, or a season of stability comes in.
2. **The Nervous System Panics.** Holding money feels unsafe or "too much."
3. **Sabotage Kicks In.** Overspending, impulsive generosity, or unnecessary risks drain the abundance.
4. **Return to Familiar Ground.** The account is empty again, but strangely, the anxiety eases. Scarcity feels "normal."

This cycle reinforces itself until abundance is redefined—not as a threat, but as a safe and natural state.

Healing Abundance Anxiety

The first step in healing is separating authentic generosity from guilt-driven giving. Sharing wealth can be beautiful when it comes from a place of overflow and alignment, not compulsion or fear.

The second step is rewriting the internalized scripts:

- Instead of *"If I don't share, I'm selfish,"* try: *"I can share when I choose to, but my needs matter too."*
- Instead of *"If I have more, I'm greedy,"* try: *"Having more allows me to create stability and opportunities for myself and others."*
- Instead of *"I should be grateful and not ask for more,"* try: *"Gratitude and desire can coexist—I can be thankful and still grow."*

Abundance does not have to equal guilt. It can mean safety, possibility, and freedom.

Redefining "Enough"

Enough is not dangerous. Enough is not greedy. Enough is a state of balance where needs are met, and growth is possible. Healing abundance anxiety means allowing yourself to rest in the space of enough without guilt, fear, or compulsion to destroy it.

Abundance is not about excess; it is about permission. Permission to feel safe. Permission to receive. Permission to hold without apology.

Reflection & Practice

1. **Memory Check-In:** Recall a time when you had "more than enough"—whether money, food, or possessions. How did others respond? Were you praised, shamed, or pressured to share? Write down what you remember.
2. **Body Awareness:** Think of having a savings cushion or extra income. Where do you feel it in your body? Notice any tension, guilt, or resistance.
3. **Rewrite the Script:** Choose one programmed phrase you grew up with (like *"If you don't share, you're selfish"*). Write a new, empowering version of that phrase that supports abundance without guilt.

Chapter 3: The Inherited Scarcity Mindset

Scarcity is not just an economic condition; it is a mindset, a way of perceiving the world that becomes imprinted through generations. Even when material resources improve, the programming of scarcity often lingers. It is the inner voice that says *"There will never be enough,"* even when there is.

Scarcity thinking does not arise in isolation. It is inherited—from schools, from parents and grandparents, and from the environments we grew up in. To heal money wounds, we must first recognize how these systems of belief became the soil in which our sense of lack was planted.

The Classroom of Scarcity

Schools, for many, are the first structured environment outside the home. And they are often steeped in subtle poverty lessons:

- **Grades as Scarce Resources.** Children are taught that success is limited—that only a few can earn "A's" or rise to the top. Abundance of learning is available, but the system frames achievement as competition.
- **The "Sharing" Script.** Students are told, *"If you don't share, you're selfish,"* but rarely taught boundaries or self-preservation. The unspoken rule: holding onto what's yours is wrong.
- **Shame Around Wealth.** Children from wealthier families may be mocked as "spoiled," while children from poorer families are told to "be grateful and not ask for more." Both messages reinforce fear of standing out financially.
- **Obedience Over Creativity.** Schools often prioritize conformity over innovation. Poverty of imagination leads to poverty of possibility. Students learn: *"Don't think too big. Stay in line."*

The result? School can condition children to view abundance as unsafe, success as limited, and individuality as threatening.

Parental Scarcity Scripts

Parents, even with love, often pass down scarcity patterns they themselves inherited. Their words and choices shape the financial "truths" we internalize:

- **"Money doesn't grow on trees."** A phrase meant to teach responsibility, but one that plants the idea that money is nearly impossible to come by.
- **"We can't afford that."** Repeated often, this becomes a child's unconscious mantra, even when finances improve later in life.
- **"Be grateful for what you have."** Gratitude is healthy, but when framed as dismissal, it equates desire with selfishness.
- **"People like us don't have money."** This identity-level belief creates self-sabotage anytime you attempt to step outside the generational script.

Parents may not intend harm. They are usually repeating what was said to them. But every statement embeds a worldview: that money is scarce, that security is temporary, that you should never expect too much.

Grandparent Echoes and Generational Trauma

Generational memory carries the weight of collective hardship—wars, depressions, recessions, systemic inequities. Many grandparents lived through eras where survival meant rationing, hoarding, and distrust of abundance. Their stories and habits ripple forward:

- A grandmother hiding cash in jars because banks "can't be trusted."
- A grandfather refusing to spend money even when needs were dire, fearing tomorrow's collapse.
- Families keeping "just enough" and discouraging risk-taking, instilling the belief that safety lies only in smallness.

These legacies are not just anecdotes; they are emotional imprints. They form an inherited nervous system response: scarcity as the default state.

Environmental Conditioning

Beyond family and school, environment reinforces scarcity:

- **Neighborhood Narratives.** If everyone around you struggled, you internalized struggle as normal.
- **Community Codes.** In some circles, success is met with suspicion—those who "make it out" are accused of forgetting their roots.
- **Media Messages.** Advertisements thrive on scarcity psychology, training people to believe they are always one purchase away from fulfillment.

Scarcity becomes atmospheric. You breathe it in without noticing, until it colors every financial decision you make.

The Scarcity Loop

Inherited scarcity thinking tends to follow a predictable loop:

1. **Expectation of Lack.** You assume resources will run out.
2. **Fear of Loss.** Even when abundance arrives, you feel unsafe holding it.
3. **Sabotage.** You unconsciously drain or reject wealth to return to the "comfort zone" of scarcity.
4. **Confirmation.** Struggle returns, proving the inherited belief correct.

This loop can last a lifetime unless challenged.

Breaking the Chain

Healing inherited scarcity does not mean rejecting your roots. It means honoring the experiences of parents and grandparents while refusing to be bound by their fears. You can thank them for their survival wisdom *and* choose a new financial story.

Questions to ask yourself:

- Which phrases about money did I hear most often growing up?
- Whose voice do I still hear when I make financial choices—my parents, my teachers, my community?
- Do these voices belong to my truth, or are they echoes of a different era?

Abundance does not dishonor your family. It can be a continuation of their survival—transformed into thriving.

Reflection & Practice

1. **Family Phrases:** Write down the top three money-related phrases you remember hearing from your parents or grandparents. Next to each one, ask: *Does this belief still serve me today?*
2. **School Conditioning:** Recall a school moment where you were praised or shamed about money, sharing, or achievement. How does that memory still shape your financial choices?
3. **Rewrite Your Inheritance:** Draft a new "family phrase" you wish had been passed down—something empowering like *"We always have enough, and we know how to grow more."* Keep it somewhere visible.

Chapter 4: Sabotage Patterns: Why We Break What We Build

We all dream of stability—steady income, a safe home, freedom from constant financial worry. Yet for many, the moment they begin to build that reality, something inside them shatters it. The raise leads to overspending. The debt payoff is followed by new debt. The opportunity is sabotaged before it can mature.

This isn't laziness, and it isn't stupidity. It is sabotage. And sabotage is often an unconscious survival pattern wired into us through fear, scarcity, and inherited trauma.

When stability feels foreign, the psyche works overtime to restore the familiar—even if the familiar is struggle.

The Psychology of Sabotage

Sabotage is not a conscious choice. Nobody wakes up and says: *Today I will ruin the progress I've worked for.* It happens beneath awareness, driven by deep-seated beliefs like:

- *"I don't deserve this."*
- *"This won't last anyway."*
- *"If I keep this, someone will take it from me."*
- *"Success makes me a target."*

These beliefs create a kind of *emotional thermostat.* Just as a thermostat adjusts the room temperature to maintain balance, sabotage resets your life back to the level of struggle you unconsciously believe is safe.

Common Sabotage Patterns

1. **Overspending as Relief.**
   When money accumulates, it can create unbearable anxiety. Spending becomes a way to discharge that tension. The brain says: *If I get rid of it, I don't have to fear losing it.*
2. **Sudden Quitting.**
   A job or project becomes too successful, too visible, or too stable. Instead of leaning in, the subconscious urges escape. Walking away restores the "safety" of uncertainty.
3. **Crisis Creation.**
   Arguments, accidents, or poor decisions are unconsciously manufactured when life is calm. Chaos reintroduces the adrenaline the body associates with "normal."
4. **Invisible Ceiling.**
   Some people stop themselves from earning above a certain threshold. The moment income climbs higher than the number tied to their self-image, they sabotage to pull it back down.
5. **Neglect of Growth.**
   Avoiding opportunities, procrastinating, or failing to follow through ensures success never fully takes root. Abundance is always "almost" but never realized.

The Emotional Logic of Sabotage

At first glance, sabotage seems irrational. But beneath it lies a twisted emotional logic:

- **Control Through Destruction.** Losing money unexpectedly feels terrifying. Losing it by choice (through overspending, quitting, or neglect) feels strangely empowering. At least *you* controlled the loss.
- **Avoiding Guilt.** Success may feel like betrayal of family or peers who still struggle. Sabotage "proves" loyalty to them.
- **Fear of the Fall.** It can feel safer never to climb high than to risk falling. Sabotage prevents the imagined devastation of future collapse.

In other words, sabotage is a strategy—an unconscious attempt to stay safe by staying small.

Case Examples of Breaking What We Build

- **The Payoff and the Spending Spree.** A man pays off $10,000 in credit card debt, only to celebrate with a vacation he can't afford—reentering debt within months.
- **The Invisible Ceiling.** A woman earns a promotion that doubles her salary. Within a year, she quits under the pressure of "not belonging," returning to a lower-paying job where she feels comfortable again.
- **The Business That Never Launches.** A creator spends years preparing a project—building, designing, researching—yet "accidentally" sabotages the launch by missing deadlines, skipping marketing, or never pressing publish.

Each of these scenarios looks different on the surface, but at their core, they are attempts to protect the self from the danger of abundance.

Recognizing Your Sabotage Style

The first step in dismantling sabotage is recognizing your own pattern. Ask yourself:

- Do I tend to drain money quickly after I earn or save it?
- Do I create drama or conflict when life feels calm?
- Do I set goals but abandon them when success is near?
- Do I secretly feel guilty when I get ahead of others?

These questions are not meant for judgment, but for clarity. Awareness transforms sabotage from an unconscious pattern into a conscious choice point.

Reframing the Pattern

Sabotage is not proof of failure—it is proof of survival. It shows how hard your nervous system has worked to keep you safe in environments that felt threatening. When you recognize this, you can meet sabotage with compassion rather than shame.

From that place, you can begin to ask: *What would safety look like if I didn't need to destroy what I build? What new patterns could I create that allow me to keep and expand my progress?*

Healing begins when sabotage is reframed not as an enemy, but as an outdated guardian trying to protect you.

Reflection & Practice

1. **Identify Your Sabotage Pattern:** Write down the most common way you "break what you build" (overspending, quitting, procrastination, etc.).
2. **Trace the Trigger:** Recall the last time it happened. What emotions came up—fear, guilt, pressure, exposure?
3. **Rewrite the Role:** Journal this sentence: *"Sabotage was trying to protect me by..."* Fill in the blank. This reframes sabotage as survival, allowing you to begin creating healthier strategies of protection.

Chapter 5: The Trauma of Stability Collapse

For many, the deepest financial wounds do not come from moments of lack, but from the collapse of stability. It is not the hunger itself, but the memory of a pantry once full and suddenly empty. It is not the unpaid bill, but the shame of losing a home that once felt secure. Stability, when gained and then ripped away, leaves scars far more complex than simple scarcity ever could.

This is the trauma of stability collapse: the shattering of trust that "enough" can last.

Why Collapse Hurts More Than Scarcity

Growing up broke can be difficult, but the nervous system adapts to it. If you never expect safety, you stop relying on it. But when stability arrives—whether in the form of steady income, a safe home, or financial security—your body begins to relax, trust, and build hope.

When that stability collapses, the betrayal cuts deeper than the original scarcity. The mind whispers: *"I was foolish to trust. I should have known better."* The nervous system learns not only to fear poverty, but to fear hope itself.

Collapse trauma teaches you that it is not safe to settle into abundance—because abundance is temporary, fragile, and always waiting to be stolen.

The Nervous System After Collapse

Psychologically, stability collapse often produces symptoms similar to post-traumatic stress:

- **Hypervigilance.** Constantly scanning for signs that safety will vanish again.
- **Suspicion of Calm.** Believing peace means danger is near.
- **Defensive Sabotage.** Destroying stability before it collapses on its own, in order to feel "in control."
- **Numbness.** Shutting down emotionally to avoid the pain of future loss.

Financial trauma is not just about money. It is about the body remembering the terror of freefall—of having the rug pulled out from under you after daring to trust the ground.

Examples of Collapse Trauma

- **The Job Loss.** Someone finally secures a high-paying role, only to be laid off months later. For years afterward, every paycheck feels temporary, every employer untrustworthy.
- **The Foreclosure.** A family buys a home, proud of their achievement, only to lose it during a downturn. The home becomes a symbol not of success, but of betrayal.
- **The Relationship Rupture.** A partner provides financial stability until a breakup shatters both the emotional and financial safety net. Future relationships carry the shadow of fear: *"It can all disappear again."*
- **The Recession Childhood.** Children of economic downturns often watch their parents go from stability to collapse overnight. These imprints remain long after the economy recovers.

Each collapse story is different, but the emotional core is the same: *I cannot trust abundance. It betrays me when I need it most.*

How Collapse Shapes Sabotage

When you've lived through collapse, sabotage begins to look less like self-destruction and more like self-protection. The logic is: *If I destroy stability myself, I will never have to endure the shock of losing it again.*

This creates cycles like:

- Spending savings before emergencies can "steal" them.
- Quitting jobs before layoffs can happen.
- Avoiding investments to prevent future crashes.

Sabotage is often a scar from collapse—an attempt to avoid reliving the pain of losing what once felt secure.

Healing the Wound of Collapse

Healing collapse trauma requires rebuilding trust—not only in money, but in yourself.

1. **Name the Loss.** Acknowledge the exact moment stability collapsed. Often, people minimize or dismiss the event, but giving it language validates the wound.
2. **Separate Past from Present.** Recognize that your nervous system is reacting to history, not to current reality. This awareness begins to release the "constant threat" cycle.
3. **Create Small Stabilizers.** Start with micro-practices: a small savings buffer, predictable routines, or a consistent habit. These small acts retrain the body to trust safety again.
4. **Rewrite the Story.** Collapse is not proof you were foolish; it is proof you were human. You trusted, you built, you invested. That act itself was strength, not weakness.

Redefining Stability

The ultimate healing lies not in pretending collapse never happened, but in redefining stability as resilient, not fragile. Stability is not a glass vase that shatters once dropped. It is a structure you can rebuild again and again, stronger each time.

When you stop fearing collapse as final, you begin to see stability as a skill—something you can create, protect, and repair.

Reflection & Practice

1. **Memory Map:** Write down the first major stability collapse you remember (job, home, relationship, recession). How old were you? What feelings did you experience at the time?
2. **Body Check-In:** Recall that event in your mind. Where does the memory live in your body—chest, stomach, throat? Breathe into that place and remind yourself: *That was then. I am here now.*
3. **Stability Reframe:** Journal this sentence: *"Stability is not fragile because I can..."* Finish with three actions you can take today to strengthen your sense of safety (e.g., save $10, create a budget, commit to self-care).

Chapter 6: Redefining Wealth Beyond Money

Wealth is often measured in dollar signs, bank balances, or possessions. From childhood, we're taught to equate money with success and stability with worth. Yet, when trauma has distorted our relationship with money, financial figures alone cannot heal the wounds. True wealth must be expanded beyond money.

Redefining wealth does not mean rejecting financial abundance—it means broadening its definition so that safety, belonging, meaning, and joy become part of the equation. When we expand what wealth means, we remove some of the fear, guilt, and sabotage attached to money itself.

Why Money Alone Feels Fragile

For those carrying money wounds, financial security feels fragile because it rests on a single pillar: numbers in an account. If that pillar collapses, everything collapses with it.

But when wealth is reframed to include relationships, health, knowledge, creativity, spirituality, and community, abundance becomes more resilient. Even if one pillar wavers, others remain standing.

This is not to minimize financial security. Money matters. It buys safety, freedom, and opportunity. But when money is the *only* definition of wealth, it becomes overburdened—carrying expectations it cannot meet.

The Dimensions of True Wealth

1. **Relational Wealth.**
   The people you can call in moments of joy or crisis. True wealth is not only who shows up when you win, but who stays when you lose.
2. **Health Wealth.**
   The ability to move, breathe, and live without chronic crisis in your body. For many, health is the silent currency that only reveals its value when lost.
3. **Knowledge and Skills.**
   Skills that cannot be taken away are a form of wealth. A savings account can vanish, but the ability to create, problem-solve, and adapt is enduring abundance.
4. **Time and Freedom.**
   The ability to shape your day, to rest, to choose how your hours are spent—this is wealth many with large bank accounts never experience.
5. **Spiritual and Creative Richness.**
   The sense of purpose, connection to meaning, or joy in creation. Wealth here is the abundance of being alive, not just surviving.
6. **Environmental Stability.**
   The safety of your home, community, or ecosystem. Feeling rooted in a place that nurtures you is a kind of wealth often overlooked.

By weaving these dimensions together, we begin to see abundance as multi-layered, not single-threaded.

Healing by Redefinition

For those who sabotage financial safety, expanding wealth beyond money can be healing. If you grew up equating money with fear, redefining wealth gives your nervous system new ways to feel abundant without panic.

- If money feels unsafe, you can still grow wealth in friendships.
- If abundance triggers guilt, you can build wealth in knowledge or time.
- If stability collapse left scars, you can anchor in health or creativity as wealth that no one can take.

This reframing softens the intensity of money as the only measure.

The Scarcity Trap of Narrow Wealth

When wealth is defined narrowly, scarcity dominates. For example:

- A person with millions but no close relationships may feel poor.
- Someone with strong health and community but low finances may be pressured to see themselves as "failing."

Both views are distortions. True abundance balances both financial and non-financial forms of wealth, removing pressure from any single measure.

Toward Abundance Integration

Redefining wealth does not mean ignoring money wounds. Instead, it integrates money with broader abundance so that financial security feels less like a fragile miracle and more like part of a larger, steady landscape.

The goal is not to reject financial abundance, but to reclaim it as one thread in a rich tapestry. Wealth becomes a network, not a single point of failure.

Reflection & Practice

1. **Inventory of Wealth:** Make a list of your current "wealth pillars"—financial, relational, health, time, knowledge, creativity, spirituality, environment. For each, note one way you are already wealthy.
2. **Reframe Scarcity:** Choose one area where you feel lack. Ask: *If money is not the only form of wealth, what kind of abundance already exists here?*
3. **Integration Journal:** Write this sentence and complete it three times: *"I am wealthy because..."* Do not mention money. Focus on other forms of abundance.

Chapter 7: Building Capacity for Peace

Peace sounds simple—something everyone should welcome without hesitation. Yet for those who carry money wounds and trauma around abundance, peace itself can feel intolerable. Stillness can feel like a trap. Calm can stir suspicion. When the nervous system has been trained by instability, the very absence of chaos can create discomfort so sharp that people unconsciously reach for sabotage.

Building capacity for peace is therefore not about learning how to "relax" in a shallow sense. It is about retraining your body and mind to tolerate the safety and calm that wealth—financial or otherwise—makes possible. Without this capacity, peace will continue to feel fleeting, unnatural, and undeserved.

Why Peace Feels Dangerous

When life has been defined by survival, peace is an unfamiliar state. The body grows accustomed to adrenaline, to hypervigilance, to problem-solving at all times. Calm is not neutral; it is threatening, because calm often preceded collapse.

- **In childhood instability,** silence may have meant danger was brewing.
- **In financial struggle,** moments of stability may have been followed by sudden loss.
- **In abusive environments,** peace was often the fragile pause before an outburst.

Over time, the nervous system encodes this pattern: peace = danger. So when safety finally arrives, it feels intolerable.

The Nervous System and Capacity

Think of the nervous system like a container. If your container was shaped in chaos, it can only hold so much calm before it spills over into anxiety. Expanding capacity means gradually stretching that container so peace can be held without panic.

Signs your peace capacity is low:

- You feel restless or uneasy when things are going well.
- You start "waiting for the other shoe to drop."
- You pick fights, overspend, or self-sabotage during calm periods.
- You minimize your wins, as if joy must be quickly diluted.

Recognizing these signals is the first step toward expansion.

Practices for Expanding Peace Capacity

1. **Micro-Doses of Calm.**
   Instead of expecting yourself to "relax" for long stretches, practice peace in tiny doses. A slow breath. A quiet cup of tea. A moment of gratitude. These micro-practices begin to train the nervous system that calm can be safe.
2. **Anchor in the Body.**
   Trauma often lives in the body. Place your hand on your chest or stomach when calm arises and remind yourself: *This peace belongs to me. I am safe here.* Over time, the body begins to associate peace with ownership, not danger.
3. **Replace Anticipation with Acknowledgment.**
   Instead of waiting for peace to end, acknowledge its presence in real time: *Right now, I am safe. Right now, I have enough. Right now, I can rest.* This builds presence instead of projection.
4. **Create Predictable Rhythms.**
   Chaos is often cyclical; peace can be too. Building small rituals—weekly budgeting, daily reflection, consistent meals—signals to the nervous system that stability is sustainable, not accidental.
5. **Celebrate Without Fear.**
   Many downplay abundance for fear it will disappear. Instead, practice celebrating wins—even small ones—without apology. Joy itself expands peace capacity.

The Myth of Constant Crisis

Part of building peace capacity is dismantling the internal myth that life must be lived in constant crisis. The survival system thrives on adrenaline, but true abundance thrives on consistency.

Ask yourself: *Do I subconsciously believe that only through struggle do I prove my worth? Do I equate being busy, anxious, or overextended with being responsible?* If so, peace will always feel threatening, because it dismantles the identity of "the struggler."

Peace requires not just nervous system work, but identity work—the willingness to see yourself as someone who deserves ease.

Peace as Wealth

Redefining wealth beyond money (as in the last chapter) is incomplete without peace. Peace is not the absence of problems; it is the presence of enough safety to handle them without collapse. Peace is wealth in its purest form: the wealth of time, breath, and presence.

When you can hold peace, abundance becomes less frightening. You no longer need chaos to feel alive, or scarcity to feel familiar. Instead, peace becomes your baseline—something you can expand, nurture, and protect.

Reflection & Practice

1. **Peace Tolerance Scan:** Recall the last time you felt genuine calm. How long did it take before restlessness, guilt, or anxiety arose? Write about what happened internally.
2. **Micro-Practice Commitment:** Choose one 2–5 minute ritual (breathing, tea, journaling, stretching) to practice daily for the next week. Notice how your body reacts to these pockets of calm.
3. **Identity Reframe:** Write this sentence and finish it three times: *"I am someone who deserves peace because..."* Allow your answers to stretch beyond money into worth, health, and belonging.

Chapter 8: Anchoring Abundance Without Fear

Abundance is not only about achieving wealth—it is about learning to hold it without panic. For those carrying money wounds, abundance itself can feel unstable, heavy, or even threatening. When you've been wired by scarcity or collapse, receiving more than "just enough" activates alarm bells. Fear of loss, guilt of having, or anxiety of being seen can overwhelm the joy of abundance.

Anchoring abundance means creating roots deep enough to hold wealth, security, and prosperity without being swept back into sabotage or collapse. It is about teaching the body and mind that abundance is not an intruder to fear, but a state you can safely live in.

Why Abundance Feels Unsafe

To understand why abundance must be anchored, we must first explore why it feels unsafe in the first place.

1. **Fear of Loss.** Having more increases the perceived risk of losing more. A small fall feels survivable; a great fall feels catastrophic.
2. **Guilt Programming.** Many were taught that having more makes you greedy, ungrateful, or selfish. Abundance is unconsciously linked to shame.
3. **Visibility Anxiety.** Having wealth or stability can make you feel exposed. Others might envy, judge, or resent you. Staying small feels safer.
4. **Unfamiliar Nervous System State.** If your body equates safety with instability, holding abundance feels overwhelming—like carrying more than your system can handle.

Unless these associations are addressed, abundance will always trigger fear rather than peace.

Anchoring as Nervous System Training

Anchoring abundance is not about forcing yourself to "just relax." It is about slowly building the capacity to stay present when abundance is present. Think of it as training your nervous system to tolerate more wealth, more calm, and more stability without reverting to sabotage.

Strategies include:

- **Gradual Exposure.** Increase what you hold slowly—saving a small cushion, allowing money to sit in your account without rushing to spend it.
- **Somatic Anchors.** Pair moments of abundance with grounding practices: deep breaths, body awareness, or touching a physical object (like a stone, necklace, or journal) to remind yourself you are safe.
- **Consistent Rituals.** Create small routines around abundance—weekly check-ins with your bank account, gratitude lists, or mindful spending rituals. Consistency signals to the nervous system that abundance is sustainable.

Shifting the Story of Abundance

Abundance cannot be anchored if it is tied to negative meanings. To reframe abundance:

- Replace *"If I have more, I am greedy"* with *"When I have more, I can support myself and others responsibly."*
- Replace *"I will lose it all if I relax"* with *"Stability is something I can nurture and grow."*
- Replace *"I don't deserve this"* with *"I am learning to deserve peace and plenty."*

Language rewires identity. Anchoring requires rewriting the story of what abundance means in your life.

Practical Anchoring Practices

1. **The Holding Exercise.** Each time you receive income, resist the urge to move it instantly. Let it sit in your account for a day or two while you breathe and notice the sensations it brings up. The practice is not about the money—it's about teaching your body that holding abundance is safe.
2. **Abundance Object.** Choose a physical item (a coin, a stone, a ring) to represent wealth. Hold it during moments of anxiety about money. Anchor abundance in a tangible form that can travel with you.
3. **Safety Statements.** Create a short mantra like *"Abundance is safe with me"* or *"I can hold wealth without fear."* Repeat it each time fear arises.
4. **Celebrate Without Collapse.** Allow yourself to celebrate wins—big or small—without diminishing them. Anchoring abundance means normalizing joy, not rushing to the next crisis.

Abundance as a Stable Identity

When abundance is only seen as luck, chance, or a fleeting season, it cannot be anchored. Anchoring means shifting from *"I have abundance right now"* to *"I am someone who can live in abundance safely."*

This shift turns abundance from an external condition into an internal identity. Anchoring is less about what you have and more about who you are becoming.

Reflection & Practice

1. **Abundance Tolerance Test:** Write down how much money or stability you feel comfortable holding before you start feeling restless or anxious. Notice if that number is lower than what you actually need to thrive.
2. **Anchor Creation:** Choose one somatic anchor (like a stone, journal, or gesture) to symbolize safety with abundance. Use it during financial check-ins.
3. **Rewrite Your Script:** Journal this sentence three times: *"Abundance is safe because..."* Complete it with different endings each time.

Chapter 9: Success Without Sabotage

Success should feel like freedom—the culmination of hard work, persistence, and vision. Yet for many carrying money wounds, success feels like a trap. The moment things start going well, fear creeps in: *What if I lose it? What if others resent me? What if I'm not strong enough to sustain this?*

These fears activate sabotage cycles. Opportunities are abandoned, savings are drained, or conflicts are created. Instead of enjoying success, it becomes a stage set for collapse. To heal, we must learn how to experience success without sabotaging it—how to let prosperity expand instead of unravel.

The Hidden Beliefs Behind Sabotage

Sabotage thrives on deeply rooted, often unconscious beliefs:

1. **"I don't deserve this."** Success feels unearned, leading to guilt-driven behaviors that give it away or push it away.
2. **"This won't last."** If success is assumed temporary, sabotage feels like bracing for the inevitable fall.
3. **"If I rise, I'll be rejected."** Fear of envy, judgment, or abandonment by peers can lead to shrinking back into struggle.
4. **"If I succeed, I'll lose myself."** Many fear that success will change them, making them greedy, arrogant, or disconnected.

Unless these beliefs are uncovered and challenged, success will never feel safe enough to hold.

Recognizing Sabotage in Action

Sabotage does not always look like dramatic destruction. It often wears subtle disguises:

- **Procrastination:** Putting off key steps just as momentum builds.
- **Overgiving:** Draining resources by giving away too much, too soon.
- **Sudden Quitting:** Leaving jobs, projects, or relationships when they become stable.
- **Overspending:** Using windfalls or raises as excuses to spend recklessly.
- **Conflict Creation:** Picking fights or making chaotic choices to reintroduce instability.

The pattern is less about what happens and more about *when* it happens: sabotage tends to appear at the threshold of growth.

Reframing Success as Safe

To stop sabotage, success must be reframed as a safe, natural state rather than an alien or threatening one. This involves three shifts:

1. **From Luck to Identity.** Success is not a fluke—it is an expression of who you are and the choices you make.
2. **From Isolation to Connection.** Success does not have to separate you from others; it can connect you through mentorship, inspiration, or generosity.
3. **From Fragility to Skill.** Success is not something to "hold onto" tightly—it is something you learn to manage and grow like a skill.

When success becomes part of your identity, relationships, and skillset, sabotage loses its power.

Practices for Success Without Sabotage

1. **Name Your Ceiling.** Everyone has an internal "success ceiling"—a point where progress feels "too much." Write down the exact point where you feel triggered (a certain savings amount, job title, income level). This awareness is the first step to expansion.
2. **Create Safety Rituals Around Growth.** Pair financial or career wins with grounding practices. For example, when you receive a raise, spend time journaling about safety before spending. Anchor growth in calm, not chaos.
3. **Celebrate Incrementally.** Instead of overwhelming yourself with one large leap, celebrate small wins regularly. This rewires the brain to associate growth with safety and joy, not fear.
4. **Practice Receiving Without Giving Back Immediately.** Many sabotage success by rushing to "balance the scales." Practice receiving—praise, money, opportunities—without reflexively overgiving.
5. **Rehearse Success.** Visualize not only achieving your goal but living with it comfortably. See yourself keeping wealth, sustaining relationships, and remaining grounded.

The Nervous System of Success

Success, like abundance, requires nervous system expansion. If your body is accustomed to crisis, success feels overstimulating. Building capacity for peace (Chapter 7) and anchoring abundance (Chapter 8) lay the groundwork for success to feel natural.

Practical nervous-system practices include:

- Slowing down decision-making when new opportunities arrive.
- Pausing before reacting to financial gains.
- Breathing deeply and grounding when fear of "too much" arises.

These practices prevent impulsive sabotage and allow success to integrate gradually.

Redefining What Success Means

Success must also be personally redefined. If you've inherited definitions of success that clash with your values, sabotage may actually be protecting you from living a life that feels false.

Ask yourself:

- *Does my version of success feel authentic or borrowed?*
- *Am I chasing someone else's definition, or my own?*
- *What kind of success feels both abundant and peaceful to me?*

When success aligns with your values, sabotage loses its purpose.

Reflection & Practice

1. **Success Ceiling Journal:** Write down the level of success (income, achievement, or stability) where you usually begin sabotaging. What fears surface at that point?
2. **Reframe a Fear:** Choose one belief (like *"If I succeed, people will resent me"*) and rewrite it as an empowering statement (*"If I succeed, I inspire others to grow too"*).
3. **Safe Success Visualization:** Close your eyes and imagine yourself living in success without sabotage. Notice what it feels like in your body to hold that safely.

Chapter 10: Safe Prosperity Practices

Healing money wounds is not just about insight—it is about practice. Awareness breaks the cycle of sabotage, but habits create safety. Prosperity must be lived in ways that feel sustainable to the nervous system, aligned with your values, and consistent enough to anchor stability.

Safe prosperity practices are not quick fixes or rigid formulas. They are gentle, repeatable actions that tell your body and mind: *I am safe with abundance. I can hold and grow prosperity without fear.*

Why "Safe" Prosperity Matters

Traditional financial advice often emphasizes growth, risk, and discipline. While useful, this approach can feel overwhelming for those with money trauma. Safety must come first. Without safety, prosperity feels fragile, triggering the same sabotage patterns we've already explored.

When prosperity is practiced safely, it becomes a source of calm rather than chaos. You begin to trust not only money, but yourself in relationship to it.

Core Elements of Safe Prosperity

1. **Predictability.** Safety thrives in rhythm. Regular routines around money create stability, reducing the shock of sudden decisions.
2. **Gentle Expansion.** Instead of massive leaps, prosperity grows through small, sustainable steps that the nervous system can tolerate.
3. **Embodiment.** Safe prosperity is felt in the body. Practices should not only manage money but also calm the nervous system.
4. **Alignment.** Prosperity must reflect your values—otherwise, sabotage will eventually reject it as "unsafe."

Daily Practices

1. **The Grounded Check-In.**
   Spend 5–10 minutes each morning or evening reviewing your finances—not as a test, but as a ritual. Pair it with deep breathing or holding a grounding object. The goal is to build comfort with looking at your money consistently.
2. **The Gratitude Ledger.**
   Write down one financial "enough" moment each day: a meal paid for, a bill covered, a small luxury enjoyed. This conditions your mind to see prosperity as already present.
3. **Micro-Saving.**
   Even saving $1 builds safety. Each small act signals that you can hold abundance. The amount matters less than the ritual of keeping something.
4. **Embodied Spending Pause.**
   Before major purchases, place a hand on your chest or stomach and ask: *Does this feel safe or reactive?* This shifts spending from impulse to alignment.

Weekly Practices

1. **Prosperity Planning Session.**
   Once a week, review upcoming expenses, savings, and goals. Use this time to check in not only on numbers but also on emotions: *Do I feel anxious, calm, or guilty about money right now?* This keeps awareness integrated.
2. **Generosity with Boundaries.**
   Practice giving in small, intentional ways that do not drain you. This rewires generosity from guilt-driven to choice-driven.
3. **Celebration Ritual.**
   Each week, acknowledge one small success—paying a bill, resisting sabotage, saving a little more. Celebration normalizes growth instead of waiting for collapse.

Monthly Practices

1. **Safety Budget Review.**
   Create a "safety budget" (expanded in Appendix A) that prioritizes essentials and emotional well-being. Revisit it monthly to adjust with compassion, not shame.
2. **Wealth Beyond Money Audit.**
   Reflect on your non-financial wealth (relationships, health, time, skills). Write down where abundance already exists so money doesn't carry all the pressure.
3. **Anchor Ritual.**
   Perform a small symbolic act to "anchor" prosperity—lighting a candle, holding a prosperity object, or repeating a mantra like *"I am safe with wealth."* Repetition builds trust.

Prosperity Without Pressure

Safe prosperity is not about perfection or pushing yourself to meet extreme goals. It is about making prosperity sustainable—building habits that allow wealth to grow without activating fear or sabotage.

Ask yourself: *Does my prosperity feel safe to live in? Or do I feel like I am constantly bracing for collapse?* The practices in this chapter exist to shift prosperity from fragile to steady, from overwhelming to supportive.

The Long-Term Impact

When practiced consistently, safe prosperity habits create:

- **Trust in Self.** You begin to believe you can handle wealth responsibly.
- **Resilient Abundance.** Even if setbacks occur, your routines keep you grounded.
- **Reduced Fear.** Money becomes less charged with panic and more integrated into everyday life.
- **Room for Growth.** Once safety is established, prosperity can expand without destabilizing you.

Safe prosperity is not just about finances—it is about building a life where money supports peace instead of undermining it.

Reflection & Practice

1. **Daily Safety Ritual:** Choose one daily practice (grounded check-in, gratitude ledger, or micro-saving). Commit to it for the next 7 days. Notice what shifts.
2. **Weekly Anchor:** Create a simple prosperity ritual (like lighting a candle while reviewing your budget) to remind your nervous system that abundance is safe.
3. **Monthly Audit:** Journal about your wealth beyond money. What non-financial abundance do you already hold, and how can you celebrate it?

Chapter 11: Stabilizing the Abundant Self

Abundance is not just about money, safety, or peace—it is about identity. Until prosperity is integrated into who you *are*, it will always feel external, fragile, and temporary. The final stage of healing money wounds is stabilizing the self so abundance becomes an inner foundation rather than a fleeting condition.

Stabilizing the abundant self is not about forcing positivity or denying the reality of financial ups and downs. It is about anchoring your nervous system, beliefs, and daily practices so that abundance feels natural, trustworthy, and sustainable—even in seasons of change.

From Survival Self to Abundant Self

For many, the "survival self" dominates. This part of you is hypervigilant, suspicious of calm, and skilled at navigating scarcity. It kept you alive during instability, but it cannot lead you into long-term prosperity.

The "abundant self," in contrast, is not naïve or reckless. It recognizes that wealth is more than money, that stability is possible, and that sabotage is no longer necessary. Stabilizing this self requires acknowledging the survival self's history *without letting it dictate your future.*

The Four Anchors of an Abundant Identity

1. **Safety as a Core Value.**
   The abundant self does not chase risk recklessly, nor does it cling to scarcity out of fear. It places safety at the center of all financial decisions, ensuring peace is prioritized over panic.
2. **Enough as a Baseline.**
   Instead of living in the extremes of lack or excess, the abundant self embraces *enoughness*. Enough is not mediocrity; it is stability. It is the floor upon which growth can stand.
3. **Integration of Wealth Beyond Money.**
   The abundant self measures success in relationships, health, time, knowledge, and joy—not just dollars. This broader definition stabilizes identity even during financial shifts.
4. **Embodied Practices.**
   The abundant self is lived in the body. Breathing into calm, practicing grounding rituals, and expanding nervous system capacity are daily acts that keep abundance real.

Identity Work: Becoming Someone Who Holds Abundance

To stabilize the abundant self, you must move from "doing" abundance practices to "being" abundant:

- **Shift Language.** Replace phrases like *"I'm trying to manage money"* with *"I am someone who is safe with money."*
- **Shift Imagery.** Visualize yourself not just receiving abundance, but *living in it long-term without fear.*
- **Shift Behavior.** Align daily actions (saving, celebrating, grounding) with the self-concept of someone who naturally sustains prosperity.

Identity is stabilized when what you believe, say, and do about abundance align.

Navigating Setbacks Without Collapse

Stability does not mean perfection. Even abundant selves face setbacks—unexpected expenses, job changes, market downturns. The difference is how you relate to them:

- The survival self views setbacks as proof that abundance is unsafe.
- The abundant self views setbacks as challenges to be managed, not as identity-shattering events.

By practicing safe prosperity (Chapter 10) and anchoring abundance (Chapter 8), you create resilience. Stability becomes less about never falling and more about knowing you can rise without losing yourself.

Expanding Belonging in Abundance

Another layer of stabilization is relational. The abundant self is not isolated. It allows abundance to coexist with community, generosity, and connection. Instead of sabotaging success to stay small or relatable, the abundant self learns:

- *"I can succeed without abandoning others."*
- *"I can give without draining myself."*
- *"I can grow without guilt."*

Stability means no longer needing to choose between wealth and belonging. You hold both.

Living as the Abundant Self

When stabilized, the abundant self experiences prosperity not as a future destination, but as a present identity. You stop waiting for abundance to "arrive" and begin living as though it already exists within you. Money becomes one reflection of this truth—not the sole measure.

The abundant self is not perfect, but it is grounded. It does not sabotage when things go well. It does not collapse in the face of loss. It stabilizes, adapts, and continues.

Reflection & Practice

1. **Identity Journal:** Write the sentence: *"I am someone who..."* and finish it three times in ways that align with your abundant self (e.g., *"I am someone who is safe with wealth."*).
2. **Survival Self Dialogue:** Write a short conversation between your survival self and your abundant self. What does each say? How can they learn to coexist without sabotage?
3. **Embodiment Anchor:** Choose one grounding practice (breath, object, ritual) to serve as a daily reminder of your abundant identity. Use it consistently until it becomes second nature.

Appendix A: Emotional Safety Budget Exercise

Budgeting is often presented as a rigid numbers game—tracking income, subtracting expenses, and limiting spending. While these mechanics matter, traditional budgets rarely address the emotional realities of financial trauma. For someone with money wounds, even looking at numbers can trigger anxiety, guilt, or panic.

The **Emotional Safety Budget** is not about strict control. It is about creating a financial plan that integrates emotional well-being, safety, and nervous-system regulation. This approach ensures money serves not only your practical needs but also your sense of stability and peace.

Why Emotional Safety Matters in Budgeting

For those who grew up in scarcity, budgets often feel like punishment: reminders of limits, rules, and failure. But a safety-based budget reframes the process. Instead of *"What can't I have?"* it asks: *"What do I need to feel safe, supported, and calm?"*

This shift changes budgeting from deprivation into empowerment. A safety budget creates confidence: the knowledge that your financial plan honors both your numbers and your nervous system.

The Four Layers of an Emotional Safety Budget

1. **Survival Needs.**
   These are the non-negotiables: housing, food, utilities, transportation, healthcare. Without these, the nervous system cannot relax.
2. **Stability Anchors.**
   Predictable payments or habits that signal continuity—savings, debt payments, or insurance. These reinforce that you can sustain stability long-term.
3. **Emotional Well-Being.**
   Small investments that nurture joy, relaxation, and mental health—whether therapy sessions, a gym class, or a weekly coffee ritual. These "soft costs" are essential for nervous-system regulation.
4. **Expansion & Generosity.**
   Money set aside for growth, creativity, or giving. This layer builds trust that abundance is not just for survival but for thriving.

A budget that includes all four layers teaches your system that money is not just survival fuel—it is a tool for safety, stability, joy, and growth.

Step-by-Step Emotional Safety Budget Exercise

Step 1: Ground Yourself Before Numbers

Before looking at income or expenses, pause. Take 3–5 deep breaths. Place a hand on your chest or stomach. Remind yourself: *I am safe to look at my money. This is about building peace, not punishment.*

Step 2: List Your Survival Needs

Write down the essentials you must cover each month. Don't judge the list—just note what keeps you functioning. Examples: rent/mortgage, groceries, medications, transportation.

Step 3: Identify Stability Anchors

Add items that keep life predictable: savings contributions, insurance premiums, debt payments. These anchors create a baseline of continuity.

Step 4: Add Emotional Well-Being

Now list what makes you feel human, not just functional. A weekly yoga class, books, a therapy session, or setting aside money for a hobby. Even a small amount creates relief for your nervous system.

Step 5: Include Expansion & Generosity

Write down one way you'd like to invest in growth (education, creativity, new skills) and one way you'd like to give (charity, small acts of generosity). Even if the amounts are small, these categories tell your psyche: *I can expand. I can share.*

Step 6: Allocate Your Income

Now, distribute your actual monthly income across these four layers. Don't aim for perfection—aim for balance. If resources are tight, ensure survival needs are met, but commit to *at least one item* in well-being and expansion.

Step 7: Review Without Judgment

Look at the finished plan. Instead of asking, *Am I doing this right?* ask: *Does this budget make me feel safe, calm, and supported?* Adjust until the answer is yes.

Example: Emotional Safety Budget

Monthly Income: $2,000

- **Survival Needs:** $1,200 (Rent, groceries, utilities, bus pass)
- **Stability Anchors:** $300 (Savings $50, Debt $200, Insurance $50)
- **Emotional Well-Being:** $150 (Therapy $100, weekly coffee $20, books $30)
- **Expansion & Generosity:** $50 (Online course $30, donations $20)

This person's budget covers survival while still giving space to healing, joy, and growth—preventing the feeling that money only exists for bills and deprivation.

How This Exercise Heals Sabotage

Traditional budgets often ignore emotions, causing people to rebel or abandon them. The Emotional Safety Budget reduces sabotage by:

- Giving the nervous system predictability.
- Validating emotional needs as legitimate, not "extras."
- Allowing small doses of joy and generosity, which prevent binge-spending or guilt-driven giving.
- Creating balance between responsibility and freedom.

When money is managed with safety at its core, you are less likely to destroy stability out of fear.

Reflection & Practice

1. **Budget Check-In:** Create your own Emotional Safety Budget using the four layers. How does it feel different from traditional budgeting?
2. **Identify Missing Layers:** Which category (stability, well-being, expansion) do you tend to neglect? What small step can you add this month to strengthen it?
3. **Safety Statement:** Write a short affirmation and place it near your budget: *"My money plan creates safety and peace for me."*

Appendix B: Money Safety Somatic Practices

Money is not only a numbers issue—it is also a body issue. When money wounds run deep, financial conversations can trigger nervous-system responses as intense as danger itself. Tightness in the chest, knots in the stomach, sweating palms, racing thoughts—these are not signs of weakness; they are survival responses to past trauma.

Somatic practices help rewire the nervous system so money no longer feels like a constant threat. By anchoring safety in the body, you create the foundation to hold, manage, and grow abundance without panic or sabotage.

Why Somatic Practices Matter

Traditional financial advice focuses on logic and willpower. But trauma is not stored in logic—it is stored in the body. If your nervous system equates money with danger, no spreadsheet will override the fear. Somatic work bridges the gap, calming the body so the mind can make clear decisions.

These practices are not about forcing relaxation. They are about gradually retraining your system to associate money with safety, stability, and even empowerment.

Core Principles of Money Safety Somatics

1. **Awareness Before Action.** Always notice body responses before making money decisions.
2. **Small Doses Build Capacity.** Healing comes from gentle repetition, not intensity.
3. **Safety First.** Practices should leave you feeling more grounded, not overwhelmed.
4. **Integration Over Perfection.** The goal is not to "erase" fear but to carry money with less tension each time.

Somatic Practices for Money Safety

1. The Grounded Breath Check-In

- Sit with both feet flat on the floor.
- Inhale slowly through the nose for a count of four, feeling your belly rise.
- Hold for two counts.
- Exhale slowly through the mouth for six counts, releasing tension.
- Repeat three to five times before opening a bill, checking your bank account, or making a financial decision.

Why it works: Long exhales activate the parasympathetic nervous system, calming fight-or-flight responses.

2. The Safety Touch Anchor

- Place one hand on your chest and the other on your stomach.
- Gently press into both spots and breathe.
- As you inhale, silently say: *"I am safe to look at my money."*
- As you exhale, say: *"I can handle this."*

Why it works: Physical touch reminds the body of presence and safety, shifting attention away from panic into grounding.

3. The 5-4-3-2-1 Money Grounding Exercise
When money fear spikes:

- **5:** Name five things you can see.
- **4:** Name four things you can touch.
- **3:** Name three things you can hear.
- **2:** Name two things you can smell.
- **1:** Name one thing you can taste.

Why it works: This practice brings you back into the present moment instead of spiraling into imagined collapse or future fear.

4. The Release Ritual

- Write down a fearful money thought (e.g., *"I'll never have enough"*) on paper.
- Tear the paper slowly, breathing out as you release the belief.
- Place your hands on your thighs and imagine the fear leaving your body into the ground beneath you.

Why it works: Symbolic movement helps the nervous system process fear instead of holding it as tension.

5. The Abundance Expansion Breath

- Sit comfortably and imagine your rib cage as a container.
- With each inhale, visualize the container expanding wider to hold more safety, more peace, more prosperity.
- With each exhale, whisper gently: *"I can hold more."*
- Continue for two to three minutes.

Why it works: This practice trains the nervous system to tolerate the sensation of "more" without overwhelm.

When to Use Somatic Practices

- Before reviewing your budget or paying bills.
- After financial conflict or stressful conversations.
- When abundance arrives (a raise, a gift, a windfall) and panic rises.
- Anytime sabotage urges appear—like spending impulsively or quitting stability.

By pairing somatic practices with financial actions, you gradually train your body to stay calm and safe in the presence of money.

Long-Term Benefits

Consistent somatic work rewires the money-body connection:

- **Reduced Anxiety.** Money no longer triggers overwhelming panic.
- **Increased Capacity.** You can hold abundance without fear.
- **Clearer Decisions.** Calm bodies allow for grounded financial choices.
- **Deeper Safety.** Prosperity begins to feel like a stable home, not a threat.

Reflection & Practice

1. **Choose One Anchor:** Pick one somatic practice from this appendix. Commit to using it before every financial action for the next week.
2. **Notice the Shift:** Journal how your body responds before and after the practice. Over time, look for signs of less tension and more calm.
3. **Personalize Your Anchor:** Identify a gesture, word, or object (like a stone or necklace) that you can pair with these practices as a personal abundance anchor.

Appendix C: Journal Prompts to Manifest Abundance Thinking and Mindset

Healing money wounds requires more than budgeting and nervous-system work. It also requires reshaping the inner stories we tell ourselves about wealth, safety, and enoughness. Journaling is one of the most powerful tools for this transformation. By writing your fears, patterns, and hopes onto the page, you move them out of the shadows of the subconscious and into the light of awareness—where they can be rewritten.

These prompts are designed to help you challenge scarcity scripts, dismantle sabotage beliefs, and manifest a mindset where abundance feels safe, natural, and deserved. They are not about forcing false positivity; they are about uncovering truth, reframing fear, and building new neural pathways of prosperity thinking.

How to Use These Prompts

- **Consistency matters.** Set aside 10–15 minutes daily or weekly to explore a prompt.
- **Write without judgment.** Allow thoughts to flow freely, even if they seem contradictory or raw.
- **Engage the body.** Before journaling, take a few deep breaths or use one of the somatic practices from Appendix B to calm your nervous system.
- **Return often.** Revisiting the same prompt at different stages can reveal new insights.

Journal Prompts for Abundance Awareness

1. When do I feel most "enough" in my daily life—financially or otherwise? What makes those moments possible?
2. What does abundance look like beyond money (time, health, relationships, creativity)? How am I already wealthy in these ways?
3. Write a list of 10 things I already have that bring me peace and safety. How do these reflect abundance I've overlooked?

Journal Prompts for Releasing Scarcity

1. What phrases or money "rules" did I inherit from parents, grandparents, or school? How do they still live in me?
2. Which of those beliefs no longer serve me? Rewrite one as an empowering statement (e.g., "Money doesn't grow on trees" → "Money can flow to me in many ways").
3. When I think of holding more wealth, what fears surface? Where do I feel them in my body?

Journal Prompts for Healing Sabotage

1. Describe a time I sabotaged financial stability. What emotion was I protecting myself from in that moment?
2. What is my "success ceiling"—the point where I begin to feel unsafe with abundance? Why do I believe that ceiling exists?
3. How would my life look if I trusted myself to hold success without breaking it?

Journal Prompts for Anchoring Abundance

1. Write a letter to money as if it were a person. What would I thank it for? What boundaries would I set? What kind of relationship would I want?
2. Imagine myself five years in the future, living in safe abundance. Write a day-in-the-life journal entry from that version of me.
3. What small daily ritual (breath, gratitude, mindful spending) can I commit to as an act of anchoring abundance?

Journal Prompts for Expanding Prosperity

1. If money were limitless, what would I create, build, or contribute? What does that vision reveal about my true values?
2. How do I want to feel—not just *what I want to have*—when I think of prosperity?
3. Write three "I am" statements that reflect my abundant self (e.g., *"I am someone who is safe with wealth."*).

Closing Reflection

The purpose of these prompts is not only to explore but to reprogram. Each time you write, you are planting seeds of abundance thinking and slowly uprooting scarcity's grip. Over time, the journal becomes a mirror of transformation: evidence that you can live in prosperity without fear, sabotage, or collapse.

Practice Suggestion

Choose one prompt from each section (Awareness, Releasing, Healing, Anchoring, Expanding) to work with over the next five days. At the end of the week, review your answers and highlight the insights that feel most empowering. Rewrite those insights as affirmations to carry forward into daily life.

Message from the Author:

I hope you enjoyed this book, I love astrology and knew there was not a book such as this out on the shelf. I love metaphysical items as well. Please check out my other books:

-Life of Government Benefits

-My life of Hell

-My life with Hydrocephalus

-Red Sky

-World Domination:Woman's rule

-World Domination:Woman's Rule 2: The War

-Life and Banishment of Apophis: book 1

-The Kidney Friendly Diet

-The Ultimate Hemp Cookbook

-Creating a Dispensary(legally)

-Cleanliness throughout life: the importance of showering from childhood to adulthood.

-Strong Roots: The Risks of Overcoddling children

-Hemp Horoscopes: Cosmic Insights and Earthly Healing

- Celestial Hemp Navigating the Zodiac: Through the Green Cosmos

-Astrological Hemp: Aligning The Stars with Earth's Ancient Herb

-The Astrological Guide to Hemp: Stars, Signs, and Sacred Leaves

-Green Growth: Innovative Marketing Strategies for your Hemp Products and Dispensary

-Cosmic Cannabis

-Astrological Munchies

-Henry The Hemp

-Zodiacal Roots: The Astrological Soul Of Hemp

- **Green Constellations: Intersection of Hemp and Zodiac**

-Hemp in The Houses: An astrological Adventure Through The Cannabis Galaxy

-Galactic Ganja Guide

Heavenly Hemp

Zodiac Leaves
Doctor Who Astrology
Cannastrology
Stellar Satvias and Cosmic Indicas
Celestial Cannabis: A Zodiac Journey
AstroHerbology: The Sky and The Soil: Volume 1
AstroHerbology:Celestial Cannabis:Volume 2
Cosmic Cannabis Cultivation
The Starry Guide to Herbal Harmony: Volume 1
The Starry Guide to Herbal Harmony: Cannabis Universe: Volume 2
Yugioh Astrology: Astrological Guide to Deck, Duels and more
Nightmare Mansion: Echoes of The Abyss
Nightmare Mansion 2: Legacy of Shadows
Nightmare Mansion 3: Shadows of the Forgotten
Nightmare Mansion 4: Echoes of the Damned
The Life and Banishment of Apophis: Book 2
Nightmare Mansion: Halls of Despair
Healing with Herb: Cannabis and Hydrocephalus
Planetary Pot: Aligning with Astrological Herbs: Volume 1
Fast Track to Freedom: 30 Days to Financial Independence Using AI, Assets, and Agile Hustles
Cosmic Hemp Pathways
How to Become Financially Free in 30 Days: 10,000 Paths to Prosperity
Zodiacal Herbage: Astrological Insights: Volume 1
Nightmare Mansion: Whispers in the Walls
The Daleks Invade Atlantis
Henry the hemp and Hydrocephalus

10X The Kidney Friendly Diet
Cannabis Universe: Adult coloring book
Hemp Astrology: The Healing Power of the Stars

Zodiacal Herbage: Astrological Insights: Cannabis Universe: Volume 2

Planetary Pot: Aligning with Astrological Herbs: Cannabis Universes: Volume 2

Doctor Who: Convergence Protocol – The Replicator War

Nightmare Mansion: Curse of the Blood Moon

The Celestial Stoner: A Guide to the Zodiac

Cosmic Pleasures: Sex Toy Astrology for Every Sign

Hydrocephalus Astrology: Navigating the Stars and Healing Waters

Lapis and the Mischievous Chocolate Bar

Celestial Positions: Sexual Astrology for Every Sign

Apophis's Shadow Work Journal: **:** A Journey of Self-Discovery and Healing

Kinky Cosmos: Sexual Kink Astrology for Every Sign

Digital Cosmos: The Astrological Digimon Compendium

Stellar Seeds: The Cosmic Guide to Growing with Astrology

Apophis's Daily Gratitude Journal

Cat Astrology: Feline Mysteries of the Cosmos

The Cosmic Kama Sutra: An Astrological Guide to Sexual Positions

Unleash Your Potential: A Guided Journal Powered by AI Insights

Whispers of the Enchanted Grove

Cosmic Pleasures: An Astrological Guide to Sexual Kinks

369, 12 Manifestation Journal

Whisper of the nocturne journal(blank journal for writing or drawing)

The Boogey Book

Locked In Reflection: A Chastity Journey Through Locktober

Generating Wealth Quickly:How to Generate $100,000 in 24 Hours

Star Magic: Harness the Power of the Universe

The Flatulence Chronicles: A Fart Journal for Self-Discovery

The Doctor and The Death Moth

Seize the Day: A Personal Seizure Tracking Journal

The Ultimate Boogeyman Safari: A Journey into the Boogie World and Beyond

Whispers of Samhain: 1,000 Spells of Love, Luck, and Lunar Magic: Samhain Spell Book

Apophis's guides:Witch's Spellbook Crafting Guide for Halloween

Frost & Flame: The Enchanted Yule Grimoire of 1000 Winter Spells

The Ultimate Boogey Goo Guide & Spooky Activities for Halloween Fun

Harmony of the Scales: A Libra's Spellcraft for Balance and Beauty

The Enchanted Advent: 36 Days of Christmas Wonders

Nightmare Mansion: The Labyrinth of Screams

Harvest of Enchantment: 1,000 Spells of Gratitude, Love, and Fortune for Thanksgiving

The Boogey Chronicles: A Journal of Nightly Encounters and Shadowy Secrets

The 12 Days of Financial Freedom: A Step-by-Step Christmas Countdown to Transform Your Finances

Sigil of the Eternal Spiral Blank Journal

A Christmas Feast: Timeless Recipes for Every Meal

Holiday Stress-Free Solutions: A Survival Guide to Thriving During the Festive Season

Yu-Gi-Oh! Holiday Gifting Mastery: The Ultimate Guide for Fans and Newcomers Alike

Holiday Harmony: A Hydrocephalus Survival Guide for the Festive Season

Celestial Craft: The Witch's Almanac for 2025 – A Cosmic Guide to Manifestations, Moons, and Mystical Events

Doctor Who: The Toymaker's Winter Wonderland

Tulsa King Unveiled: A Thrilling Guide to Stallone's Mafia Masterpiece

Pendulum Craft: A Complete Guide to Crafting and Using Personalized Divination Tools

Nightmare Mansion: Santa's Eternal Eve

Starlight Noel: A Cosmic Journey through Christmas Mysteries

The Dark Architect: Unlocking the Blueprint of Existence

Surviving the Embrace: The Ultimate Guide to Encounters with The Hugging Molly

The Enchanted Codex: Secrets of the Craft for Witches, Wiccans, and Pagans

Harvest of Gratitude: A Complete Thanksgiving Guide

Yuletide Essentials: A Complete Guide to an Authentic and Magical Christmas

Celestial Smokes: A Cosmic Guide to Cigars and Astrology

Living in Balance: A Comprehensive Survival Guide to Thriving with Diabetes Insipidus

Cosmic Symbiosis: The Venom Zodiac Chronicles

The Cursed Paw of Ambition

Cosmic Symbiosis: The Astrological Venom Journal

Celestial Wonders Unfold: A Stargazer's Guide to the Cosmos (2024-2029)

The Ultimate Black Friday Prepper's Guide: Mastering Shopping Strategies and Savings

Cosmic Sales: The Astrological Guide to Black Friday Shopping

Legends of the Corn Mother and Other Harvest Myths

Whispers of the Harvest: The Corn Mother's Journal

The Evergreen Spellbook

The Doctor Meets the Boogeyman

The White Witch of Rose Hall's SpellBook

The Gingerbread Golem's Shadow: A Study in Sweet Darkness

The Gingerbread Golem Codex: An Academic Exploration of Sweet Myths

The Gingerbread Golem Grimoire: Sweet Magicks and Spells for the Festive Witch

The Curse of the Gingerbread Golem

10-minute Christmas Crafts for kids

Christmas Crisis Solutions: The Ultimate Last-Minute Survival Guide

Gingerbread Golem Recipes: Holiday Treats with a Magical Twist

The Infinite Key: Unlocking Mystical Secrets of the Ages

Enchanted Yule: A Wiccan and Pagan Guide to a Magical and Memorable Season

Dinosaurs of Power: Unlocking Ancient Magick

Astro-Dinos: The Cosmic Guide to Prehistoric Wisdom

Gallifrey's Yule Logs: A Festive Doctor Who Cookbook

The Dino Grimoire: Secrets of Prehistoric Magick

The Gift They Never Knew They Needed

The Gingerbread Golem's Culinary Alchemy: Enchanting Recipes for a Sweetly Dark Feast

A Time Lord Christmas: Holiday Adventures with the Doctor

Krampusproofing Your Home: Defensive Strategies for Yule

Silent Frights: A Collection of Christmas Creepypastas to Chill Your Bones

Santa Raptor's Jolly Carnage: A Dino-Claus Christmas Tale

Prehistoric Palettes: A Dino Wicca Coloring Journey

The Christmas Wishkeeper Chronicles

The Starlight Sleigh: A Holiday Journey

Elf Secrets: The True Magic of the North Pole

Candy Cane Conjurations

Cooking with Kids: Recipes Under 20 Minutes

Doctor Who: The TARDIS Confiscation

The Anxiety First Aid Kit: Quick Tools to Calm Your Mind

Frosty Whispers: A Winter's Tale

The Infinite Key: Unlocking the Secrets to Prosperity, Resilience, and Purpose

The Grasping Void: Why You'll Regret This Purchase

Astrology for Busy Bees: Star Signs Simplified

The Instant Focus Formula: Cut Through the Noise

The Secret Language of Colors: Unlocking the Emotional Codes

Sacred Fossil Chronicles: Blank Journal

The Christmas Cottage Miracle

Feeding Frenzy: Graboid-Inspired Recipes

Manifest in Minutes: The Quick Law of Attraction Guide

The Symbiote Chronicles: Doctor Who's Venomous Journey

Think Tiny, Grow Big: The Minimalist Mindset

The Energy Key: Unlocking Limitless Motivation

New Year, New Magic: Manifesting Your Best Year Yet

Unstoppable You: Mastering Confidence in Minutes

Infinite Energy: The Secret to Never Feeling Drained

Lightning Focus: Mastering the Art of Productivity in a Distracted World

Saturnalia Manifestation Magick: A Guide to Unlocking Abundance During the Solstice

Graboids and Garland: The Ultimate Tremors-Themed Christmas Guide

12 Nights of Holiday Magic

The Power of Pause: 60-Second Mindfulness Practices

The Quick Reset: How to Reclaim Your Life After Burnout

The Shadow Eater: A Tale of Despair and Survival

The Micro-Mastery Method: Transform Your Skills in Just Minutes a Day

Reclaiming Time: How to Live More by Doing Less

Chronovore: The Eternal Nexus

The Mind Reset: Unlocking Your Inner Peace in a Chaotic World

Confidence Code: Building Unshakable Self-Belief

Baby the Vampire Terrier
Baby the Vampire Terrier's Christmas Adventure
Celestial Streams: The Content Creator's Astrology Manual
The Wealth Whisperer: Unlocking Abundance with Everyday Actions
The Energy Equation: Maximize Your Output Without Burning Out
The Happiness Algorithm: Science-Backed Steps to Joyful Living
Stress-Free Success: Achieving Goals Without Anxiety
Mindful Wealth: The New Blueprint for Financial Freedom
The Festive Flavors of New Year: A Culinary Celebration
The Master's Gambit: Keys of Eternal Power
Shadowed Secrets: Groundhog Day Mysteries
Beneath the Burrow: Lessons from the Groundhog
Spring's Whispers: The Groundhog's Prediction
The Limitless Mindset: Unlock Your Untapped Potential
The Focus Funnel: How to Cut Through Chaos and Get Results
Bold Moves: Building Courage to Live on Your Terms
The Daily Shift: Simple Practices for Lasting Transformation
The Quarter-Life Reset: Thriving in Your 20s and 30s
The Art of Shadowplay: Building Your Own Personal Myth
The Eternal Loop: Finding Purpose in Repetition
Burrowing Wisdom: Life Lessons from the Groundhog
Shadow Work: A Groundhog Day Perspective
Love in Bloom: 5-Minute Romantic Gestures
The Shadowspell Codex: Secrets of Forbidden Magick
The Burnout Cure: Finding Balance in a Busy World
The Groundhog Prophecy: Unlocking Seasonal Secrets
Nog Tales: The Spirited History of Eggnog
Six More Weeks: Embracing Seasonal Transitions
The Lumivian Chronicles: Fragments of the Fifth Dimension
Money on Your Mind: A Beginner's Guide to Wealth
The Focus Fix: Breaking Through Distraction

January's Spirit Keepers: Mystical Protectors of the Cold
Creativity Unchained: Unlocking Your Wildest Ideas in 2025
Manifestation Mastery: 365 Days to Rewrite Your Reality
The Groundhog's Mirror: Reflecting on Change
The Weeping Angels' Christmas Curse
Burrowed in Time: A Groundhog Day Journey
Heartbeats: Poems to Share with Your Valentine
Dino Wicca: The Sacred Grimoire of Prehistoric Magick
Courage of the Pride: Finding Your Inner Roar
The Lion's Leap: Bold Moves for Big Results
Healthy Hustle: Achieving Without Overworking
Practical Manifesting: Turning Dreams into Reality in 2025
Jurassic Pharaohs: Unlocking the Magick of Ancient Egypt and Dino Wicca
The Happiness Equation: Small Changes for Big Joy
The Confidence Compass: Finding Your Inner Strength
Whispers in the Hollow: Tales of the Forgotten Beasts
Echoes from the Hollow: The Return of Forgotten Beasts
The Hollow Ascendant: The Rise of the Forgotten Beasts
The Relationship Reset: Building Better Connections
Mastering the Morning: How to Win the Day Before 8 AM
The Shadow's Dance: Groundhog Day Symbolism
Cupid's Kitchen: Quick Valentine's Day Recipes
Valentine's Day on a Budget: Love Without Breaking the Bank
Astrocraft: Aligning the Stars in the World of Minecraft
Forecasting Life: Groundhog Day Reflections

Bleeding Hearts: Twisted Tales of Valentine's Terror

Herbal Smoke Revolution: The Ultimate Guide to Nature's Cigarette Alternative

Winter's Wrath: The Complete Survival Blueprint for Extreme Freezes.

The Groundhog's Shadow: A Tale of Seasons
Burrowed Insights: Wisdom from the Groundhog

Sensual Strings: The Art of Erotic Bondage
Whispered Flames: Unlocking the Power of Fire Play
Forgotten Shadows: A Guide to Cryptids Lost to Time
Six Weeks of Secrets: Groundhog Day's Hidden Messages
Shadows and Cycles: Groundhog Day Reflections
The Art of Love Letters: Crafting the Perfect Message
Romantic Getaways at Home: Turning Your Space into Paradise
Purrfect Brews: A Cat Lover's Guide to Coffee and Companionship
The Groundhog's Wisdom: Timeless Lessons for Modern Life
The Shadow Oracle: Groundhog Day as a Predictor
Emerging from the Burrow: A Journey of Renewal
The Language of Love: Learning Your Partner's Love Style
Authorpreneur: The Ultimate Blueprint for Writing, Publishing, and Thriving as an Author
Weathering the Seasons: Groundhog Day Perspectives
Valentine's Day Magic: A Guide to Romantic Rituals
The Shadow Chronicles: Stories of Groundhog Day
Love and Laughter: Fun Games for Valentine's Day
AstroRealty: Unlocking the Stars for Property Success
The Groundhog's Path: A Guide to Seasonal Balance
Groundhog Day Diaries: Reflections in the Shadow
The Groundhog's Light: Illuminating the Path Ahead
Valentine's Traditions from Around the World
AI Wealth Revolution: Unlocking the Trillionaire Mindset
Love Rekindled: Reigniting Passion in Relationships
Single and Thriving: Self-Love on Valentine's Day
Emerald Legends: Mystical Tales of Ireland
Green Alchemy: Harnessing Nature's Magic
The Hearts of Horror: A Valentine's Day Nightmare
The Leprechaun's Guide to Wealth and Wisdom
Dancing with the Sidhe: Celebrating the Otherworld

Shamrocks and Shadows: Mysteries of the Green Isle
Emerald Energy: Harnessing Luck and Growth
The Gingerbread Golem's Valentine: A Sweetheart's Guide to Love and Enchantment
The Celtic Knot: Weaving Life and Destiny
Green Fire: Elemental Magic for St. Patrick's Day
Clover Chronicles: Finding Your Inner Luck
Ireland's Mystical Creatures: A Field Guide
Gingerbread Golem's Love Almanac
Prowl and Thrive: The Lion's Guide to Success
Love Alchemy: Transforming Your Life Through Heart Energy
WORLD DOMINATION: Woman's Rule 3:The New Life
The Midnight Rose: A Guide to Lunar Love Spells
The Forbidden Letters: Writing Your Own Love Prophecy
Luck and Lore: St. Patrick's Day for Modern Mystics
The Green Path: A Pagan Celebration of Renewal
The Dark Architect's Guide to Reprogramming Reality
Prankster's Paradise: A Guide to Harmless Hijinks
Manifest Your Reality: The Law of Attraction Simplified
The TARDIS Owner's Manual: Understanding the Doctor's Ship: *A complete guide to the TARDIS, its technology, secrets, and mysteries*
Starlit Romance: Astrology Secrets for Finding True Love
The Time Lord's Atlas: A Complete Guide to the Whoniverse: *A breakdown of the locations, planets, and dimensions explored in Doctor Who*
Sweetheart Shadows: The Dark Side of Love and Attraction
February Fire: Reigniting Passion in Every Area of Life
The Self-Love Toolkit: 5 Ways to Embrace Who You Are
February Sparks: Ignite Your Dreams in 28 Days
March to Success: A 31-Day Action Blueprint
Ancient Paths: The 13 Sacred Principles of Dino Wicca

Echoes of Tomorrow: Navigating the AI Revolution
The Wellness Blueprint: Balancing Mind, Body, and Soul
Green Horizons: Sustainable Living for a Better Tomorrow
The AI Wealth Code: How to Make Millions with Automation
AI-Powered Creativity: Writing, Art, and Music for Profit
Extinction Rites: Rebirthing Your Soul Through Prehistoric Magick
Sacred Serpents tarot
Celestial Enchantment blank journal
Star Strains
Culinary Journeys: Exploring Global Flavors at Home
The Hollowvale Curse
The Hollowvale Harvest
The Egg of Transformation: Awakening Your Inner Power
Blooming Into Power: A Wiccan Guide to Spring Awakening
The Nightmare Nexus: The Third Doctor's Perilous Haunting
Digital Detox: Reclaiming Your Life in a Connected World
Ostara's Path: Walking the Spiral of Renewal
The Sacred Hare
Financial Freedom: Building Wealth in the Modern Age
Spring's Cauldron: Stirring the Waters of Change
The Hollowvale Pact
Quantum Consciousness: The Science of Reality Shifting
The Hollowvale Hunger
The Sacred Waters Within: A Witch's Guide to Hydrocephalus Magick
The Raven's Nest: Building a Life of Unshakable Stability
AI and the Human Mind: The Future of Intelligence
The Hollowvale Reckoning
Timeless Love: Building and Maintaining Lasting Relationships
The Raven's Roar: Unlocking Unstoppable Confidencc
Raven Sight: Awakening Intuition and Inner Wisdom

The Butterfly Effect: Small Changes, Big Transformations

Taming the Boogeyman: How to Conquer Your Inner Fears

The Magick of Green: Awakening Earth's Energy in You

The Entrepreneurial Mindset: Secrets to Business Success

The Hollowvale End

The Shadow Luck Ritual: Reclaiming Power from Your Dark Side

Spring Magick for Beginners: A Simple Guide to Seasonal Energy Work

Doctor Who: The Hollowvale Conundrum

The March of Miracles: Unlocking Synchronicities in Spring

Unveiling the Cosmos: A Guide to Stargazing and Space Exploration

The Ultimate Guide to Surviving an Economic Collapse

The AI Gold Rush: How to Profit from the AI Revolution

Bastet's Shadow: The Hidden Power of Feline Magick

The Bastet Codex: Unlocking the Goddess's Magickal Secrets

Purring Spells: Harnessing Bastet's Healing Frequencies

Bastet's Nine Lives: Rebirth, Transformation, and Immortality Spells

Primal Currents: Hydrocephalus Magick in the Path of Dino Wicca

The Digital Gold Rush: Mastering E-Commerce and Online Sales

Future Shock: Adapting to the Next Decade of Change

The Quantum Mindset: Think Like a Billionaire

Sacred Motherhood: Awakening the Divine Feminine Within

The Mother's Spellbook: Enchantments for Love, Protection, and Prosperity

The Witch's Guide to Parenting: Raising Empowered and Intuitive Children

The Magick of Motherhood: Reclaiming Your Power Through Rituals

The Pagan Path to Self-Love: A Goddess's Guide to Worth and Confidence
Wild Woman Magick: Unleashing Your Primal Power
The Money Magnet Blueprint: Unlocking Unlimited Wealth
Biohacking 101: Unlock Your Body's Full Potential
The Wild Father: A Pagan Guide to Strength and Wisdom
The Sacred Masculine: Unlocking Your Inner Power
The Druid's Compass
The Warrior's Mindset
The Father's Fire
Odin's Path
Ancestral Bonds
The House That Whispers
The Magician's Code
The Wild Hunt
The Green Man's Path
The Altar of Success
The Shadow and the Sword
The High Priestess's Guide to Energy Healing
The Lunar Mother
The Sacred Self-Care Grimoire
The Womb Wisdom Codex
The Wheel of the Mother
The Witch's Guide to Manifestation
The Q2 Reset
The Ultimate Guide to AI-Powered Passive Income
Escape the 9-5
AI Feline Fortunes
The Tear-Stained Grimoire
Razorblade Runes
Cemetery Sirens
The Midnight Wristwatch
The Town That Forgets

AI Horror & Creepypasta
The Hollow Frequency
The Breach Echo
The Quiet Between Worlds
The Sigil of Tharan-Khul
Summon the Vault of Y'ha'ten
The Becoming Codex
The Profit of Az'ra-nar
The Drowned Logos
Echoes of the Eldritch Will
The Deep Ledger
Necronomicon of Networth
Covenant of the Wealthwyrm
The Whisperer's Manifesto
The Rites of Azh-K'luth
The Ark of the Crawling Coin
The Tithe of Shadows
Inkheart Abyss
The Timewinds of Y'ha-nthlei
The Spiral Labyrinth of Azag-Nirrh
The Gallifreyan Heresy of the Black Pharaoh
The Psalms of Nyog-Sotha
Black Rain Alchemy
The Infinite Maw
The Entropic Blueprint
The Oracle of Sh'guul
The Book of Breach
The Drowned Saint's Testament
Dreamcraft of the Sleeper God
The Silence Market
Cthonomics: The Dark Wealth Algorithm
Invocation of the Ten-Eyed King
Wealthbound to the Wyrm Below

Become the Unnameable
Codex of the Sovereign Flame
Rituals of Relentless Becoming
The Shadow Ascends
The Eyes Beneath You
The Will That Wakes Worlds
Silence Is a Weapon
The Mirror That Screams
The Whisper Between Moments
The Mind That Devours Fear
The Myth of the Finished Self
The Architect of Your Madness
The Voice You've Buried
The Discipline of Madness
Stormborn: Awakening Your Inner Tempest
The Mind That Ate Time
Unbind Your Becoming
The Pact You Owe Yourself
The Devourer's Diet
The Acid That Carves the Path
The Tower You Must Burn
The Breath Between Worlds
Speak Like the Deep
The Labyrinth Within
The Spine of the Sea God
Rejection Is a Portal
The Crown You Refused
The Scar Is the Spell
The Lightless Flame
The Habit of Becoming Horrific
ChickenJockey Chaos
The Gatekeeper Within
You Are Not Your Name

The Compass of the Mad
The Archive of Unsent Letters
What the Mirror Can't Show You
The Knife You Needed
Worship Nothing, Become Everything
The Other Voice
The Body the World Forgot
The Vein of the Void
The Black Bone Codex
The Puzzle of the Hidden Self (Millennium Puzzle)
The Eye That Sees the Lie *(Millennium Eye)*
The Ring of Return (Millennium Ring)
The Rod of Relentless Will ***(Millennium Rod)***
The Tally of the Soul (Millennium Tauk/Necklace)
The Key to the Locked Timeline (Millennium Key)
The Scale of Sacred Decisions (Millennium Scales)
Inferno Bites: The UnOfficial Minecraft Lava Cookbook
Rot in the Attic
Prana: The Hidden Force of Your Infinite Self
The Shadow Realm Within: Transforming Darkness Into Destiny
The Borderland Collapse
Claws of Protection: Bastet's Defensive Magick
Mr. Ring-a-Ding's Madness
Yugioh Astrology: Celestial Deckcraft and Duel Destiny (2026–2027 Edition)
The Seal You Signed: Unlocking the Power You Once Feared
The Puzzle of Infinite Minds: Unlocking the Mentalism Hidden Within
The Eye That Mirrors the All: Secrets of Inner Reflection
Doctor Who: The Toymaker's Broadcast
The Rod of Eternal Flow: Commanding the Currents of Vibration

Doctor Who: The World That Froths
Rootwake: The Fizz That Rewrites Flesh
Rootwake: Frothfather of the World
The Holly Pact: Blood Beneath the Mistletoe
The 2nd Mass Principle: Building Unbreakable Tribes
Web of Wits: A Survival Guide to Encounters with Anasi the Spider (Aunt Nancy)
The Hexbreaking Handbook: Effective Spells to Remove Curses
Pop Alchemy: Transform Your Life One Sip at a Time
The Mason Code: Leading in Unleadable Times
Petosiris and the Fifth Chamber of Thoth
The Ether Seed Within
The Parent of Tomorrow
Petosiris's Pyramid of Perpetual Wealth
Unlearn the World
Grimoire of the Hollow Tongue
Zodiac Weeds: Finding Your Strain Through the Stars
Aquarius Rises in the Bank
The Sugar God's Smile
The Skinclock Reversal: Biohacking the Face of Time
Debtburn: How to Obliterate What You Owe Forever
The Ice Cream Oracle: What Your Cone Says About Your Future
Silence Is Sovereignty: The Power of Being Unreadable
The Wind That Whispers Through Stone
Path of the Four Directions
Doctor Who: The Maestro's Symphony of Endings
Oxygen Grail: Breathing to Undo the Clock
Zodiacal Collapse: When Stars Devour Time
Teachings from the Red Sand Silence
Doctor Who: Omega – The Broken Equation
Memory Wipe Your Past: Start Over Like a MiB

Mitochondria Prime: Ignite the Core of Youth
A Nest of Roaches
Grub from the Galaxy: MiB Recipes You'll Never Forget
Whiskers of Power: Bastet's Guide to Inner Sovereignty
The Gift Must Cost Them: Negotiation Through Unequal Exchange
The Worm Guys' Wealth Code: Hustle Like an Alien
Bug Out: The Edgar Method for Ruthless Goal Setting
Weaving Life with Spiderwoman's Pattern
Doctor Who: The Rani's Renaissance
How to Get a Job (If You're a Puppygirl)
Speak Through Others: The Art of Proxy Power
T-Rex Your Trauma: Reclaim the Power of Your Primal Self
The Black Briefcase: How MiB Stay Wealthy in Silence
The Thirst Beyond Reason: Understanding Diabetes Insipidus From the Inside Out
Backwoods Witchcraft for Billionaires: The Pagan Path from Dirt Roads to Gold Roads
The Moonshine Grimoire: Fermented Spells for Abundance
The Nameless Geometry
The Wraith's Mixtape: Spellcasting with Songs of Sorrow
The Gallifreyan Gentleman: Silent Wealth, Sonic Confidence, and the Doctor's Code of Living
Sugar Water Confidence
Dino Totems: Spirit Guides from Earth's First Gods
Pumpkin Sigils & Ritual Smoke
The Hózhó Compass
The Distortus Discipline – Order from Inner Mutation
Witchcraft for the Cold-Blooded Soul
Moonlight Over the Blessingway
Water, Interrupted: When the Body Forgets How to Hold On
Deformed but Divine: Embracing Your Asymmetry
Hexes in the Henhouse: The Farm Witch's Guide to Power

The Reversed Flame: A Grimoire of Inverted Power

Salt, Cells, and Sanity: Reclaiming Balance with Diabetes Insipidus

King of the Broken: Crowning the Flawed Self

Moonlight Scars: Emo Moon Magick and the Art of Lunar Sorrow

Noose Spells: Magick of the Hanging Rope

The Goth Cathedral: Rituals of the Broken and Beautiful

The Cretaceous Codex: Dino Spirits and Fossil Magick

The Turkey Bones Ritual

Nine Lives of Manifestation: Unlocking Bastet's Reality Codes

Chaos Muscles: Building Strength from Twisted Pain

Emo Blood Magick: The Veins of Power

The 3AM Flood: Nighttime Urination, Sleep Loss, and the DI Spiral

The Silence Between the Stars

The Lemon Method: Sour Your Way to Success

Starlit Sovereign

The Rite of Twelve Gates: Walking the Gates of the Duat.

Cornbread and Conjure: Recipes for Riches and Rootwork

The Black Rose Rituals: Emo Love Spells and Obsession Magick

The Eternal Goodbye: Death Magick and Rebirth Rituals

Sinkrot: The Drain That Remembers

The Hybrid Mindset: Thinking Beyond Evolution

Bone Dry: Navigating Dehydration Before It Breaks You

Wreathcraft: Winter Sigils and Yuletide Spells

The Rite of Twelve Mouths

S'mores of the Damned: Haunted Recipes for Halloween Night

Rethink the Drink: A Beverage Survival Guide for DI Warriors

The Shadow Chord: Guitar Magick and Sonic

Malformed Yet Majestic: Leading When You Feel Wrong Inside

The Cursed Diary: Ink-Stained Spells of the Emo Soul

Anxiety Off Switch: Emergency Reset for a Fried Nervous System

The Energy Heist: How to Take Back Your Life from Drainers

Beyond the Bathroom: Rebuilding Your Social Life With DI

Coyote's Gift for Decision Makers

Ghoul-Goo: Spooky S'mores You'll Die For

Echoes in the Mirror: Scrying and Self-Destruction Magick

Thread and Thorn: Stitching Spells from Rural Cloth

The Mogwai Mind: Building Untouchable Wealth from Small Ideas

Be Your Own Guide: Trust Your Inner Compass

Hormones in Chaos: The Endocrine Puzzle of Diabetes Insipidus

ChronoCleanse: Detox Your Biological Timeline

The Limb You Hide Is the One That Saves You

Leaves, Bones, and Whisper Spells

The Dinosaur Mindset: Prehistoric Tactics for Modern Wealth

Clawing Back Control: A Bastet Method for Boundaries and Empowerment

Samhain Codes of the Forgotten

Orange Alchemy: The Autumnal Spellbook

Monster Within, Master Without

The Sigil That Sleeps

Hearthcraft: Yule Hearth Sigils and Winter Warmth Spells

Temple of the Purring Moon: Rituals from Bastet's Lineage

When the Earth Remembers Your Footsteps

Food for Mood: Eat to Heal Depression, Not Just Survive It

Witch of the Kudzu Vine: Southern Pagan Wealth Secrets

The Invisible Diagnosis: Advocating for Yourself With DI

The Coffin's Lullaby: Sleep Magick and Nightmares as Portals
Ashes of the Will: Rituals for Erasing the Self
The Fracture Rite: Shattering the Magickal Core
Funeral Candles: The Art of Emo Flame Magick
The Black Grimoire: A Blank Ritual for Writing in Absence
Phantom Thirst: A Halloween Survival Guide for Diabetes Insipidus
The Hollow Crown: Emo Royalty and Magick of the Outcast King
Sandpainting for the Soul
Falling Into Balance: Using the Extra Hour to Recalibrate Life
100 Southern Superstitions That Still Work
The DI Child: A Parent's Guide to Raising Hydrated, Happy Kids
The Jungle of Shame: Escaping the Hidden Lab of Doubt
The Witch's Toast: S'mores Spells and Creepy Confections
The Hoodoo Pantry: Spells from the Mason Jar
The Immortal Fortune: Secret Wealth Lessons from Captain Jack Harkness
The Specter's Embrace: Magick for Channeling Ghostly Lovers
Grateful Waters: A Thanksgiving Survival Guide for Diabetes Insipidus
The Seizure Gospel
Harvestbind: Autumn Sigils and Samhain Spells
Doctor Who: The Algorithmic Awakening
Silent Nights, Steady Waters: A Christmas Survival Guide for Diabetes Insipidus
The Extra Hour Effect: How One Hour Can Transform Everything
Blade Between the Breaths
Running with the Mountain Shadows
Echoes of the Failed Experiment – Becoming a Living Legacy

Swamp Witches & River Ghosts: Real Southern Hauntings

Cornbread Prophecies: Magical Recipes from a Southern Table

Doctor Who: The Signal in the Star

Bloomcraft: Spring Sigils and Equinox Enchantments

Vanisher: How to Disappear from the Internet Without Losing Your Life

The Ultimate Christmas Cookie Cookbook

The Unbreakable Parent: How to Mentally Survive Raising Kids in a Broken World

Time Debt: How to Reclaim the Hours You Didn't Know You Lost

One Month, One Million: Unconventional Cash Creation Tactics

Doctor Who: The Cyber Conversion Protocol

Black Friday Frenzy: The Art of Finding Hidden Online Deals

The Grimoire Buried Under the Apple Tree

Digital Couponing Masterclass: Your Step-by-Step Guide to Black Friday Savings

The Fire Inside the Flint

Shadows on the Ceiling: The Emo Guide to Astral Magick

The Bone-Eaters Beneath Us

Black Friday Bundle Blueprint: Creating Irresistible Product Packages for Maximum Sales

Thirteen Nights of Unbinding

Doctor Who: Engines of Influence

Pumpkin Spice Alchemy: Recipes of Fire and Frost

When Raptor Met Rexy: Prehistoric Lessons in Wild Romance

Oblivion's Candle: Burn the Path Behind You

Campfire Curses and Chocolate: A Halloween S'mores Grimoire

The Wallet That Wasn't Mine: Breaking Free from Inherited Scarcity

The Cola Zodiac: What Your Fizz Says About Your Fate

Frostfire Fortune: Unlocking Winter's Hidden Prosperity

Signal Jamming: Detox Your Brain from Info Overload

The Dust of the Forgotten Rite

The Golden Cat Sigils: Drawing Power in Bastet's Name

Mud Magick: The Prosperity of Getting Dirty

Savory Spicefall: Beyond the Pumpkin Pie

Pumpkin Spice Apothecary Kitchen

The Pumpkin Spice Economy: Turning Trends into Billions

The Ember Veil: 13 Nights of Fire Magick

Financial Freeze: When Earning Triggers Panic

The Gingerbread Alchemist: Sweet Recipes with a Twist

Biosynth Power: Programming Yourself from Scratch

Echoes from the Talking Circle

Truffle Alchemy: Fungus of Fortune

Spores of Power: The Truffle Witch's Handbook

Doctor Who: The Tower That Speaks

The Mycelium Veil: Truffle Magick Unbound

Broke But Ashamed: Healing the Shame Wound of Debt

The Evergreen Mind: Growth Through Winter Stillness

The Black Veil Truffle Rite

The Voice Beneath Symbols

Witchlight on the Bayou: Swamp Spells for Sovereignty

I Grew Up Poor and Now I Sabotage My Success

The Lantern of Hollow Souls

Shutdown Survival: A Citizen's Guide to Thriving When Government Stops

Get Some Tarot cards: https://www.makeplayingcards.com/sell/apophis-occult-shop

Get some shirts: https://www.bonfire.com/store/apophis-shirt-emporium/

<u>Instagrams:</u>
@apophis_enterprises,
@apophisbookemporium,
@apophisscardshop
Twitter: @apophisenterpr1
Tiktok:@apophisenterprise
Youtube: @sg1fan23477
Hive: @sg1fan23477
CheeLee: @SG1fan23477

Podcast: Apophis Chat Zone: https://open.spotify.com/show/5zXbrCLEV2xzCp8ybrfHsk?si=fb4d4fdbdce44dec

Newsletter: https://apophiss-newsletter-27c897.beehiiv.com/

If you want to support me or see posts of other projects that I have come over to: **buymeacoffee.com/mpetchinskg**

I post there daily several times a day

Get your Dinowicca or Christmas themed digital products, especially Santa Raptor songs and other musics. Here: **https://sg1fan23477.gumroad.com**

Apophis Yuletide Digital has not only digital Christmas items, but it will have all things with Dinowicca as well as other Digital products.

www.ingramcontent.com/pod-product-compliance
Lightning Source LLC
LaVergne TN
LVHW022005200926
848481LV00007B/2250
* 9 7 9 8 3 4 9 5 9 9 8 3 5 *